THE LITTLE BOOK OF

quick fixes
FOR THE IMPATIENT
GARDENER

Gay Search

Quadrille

Contents

4 Introduction
6 Walls and fences
50 At ground level
120 Containers
156 Lighting
176 Arches and arbours
198 Furniture
210 Water
226 Features
244 Plant magic
286 Keeping it going

302 Index
304 Acknowledgements

Introduction

We live in an age of instant gratification. We can have what we want almost the moment we decide that we want it, whether it's a microwave meal or a takeaway, an online air ticket or the latest DVD from a website. Patience, it seems, is no longer a virtue.

The same is true when it comes to gardening. Many of us don't have time to garden, let alone wait for our garden to mature. We lead busy lives so we want to enjoy our gardens primarily by relaxing in them, not by slaving away. It's hardly surprising then that many of us are impatient gardeners too.

My *Little Book of Quick Fixes for the Impatient Gardener* is the answer. Its pages are packed with bite-size pieces of sound advice, tips and ideas that are accessible to even the most sceptical of impatient gardeners.

Throughout, you'll find the emphasis is on the impatient gardener, with ideas that give you maximum drama for minimum effort. I even include my very own Impatient Gardener's Question Time questions and answers!

Dip inside to find a host of easy, small-scale garden projects to do in a couple of hours – or a weekend at most – together with speedy garden fixes and planting ideas for instant results and long-term pleasure. And once you have the garden of your dreams, read my tips on how to keep it looking good all year long.

No matter whether your garden is cricket-pitch size or just a window box, you'll find my book is all you need to make your own private paradise – and in record time!

Gay Search

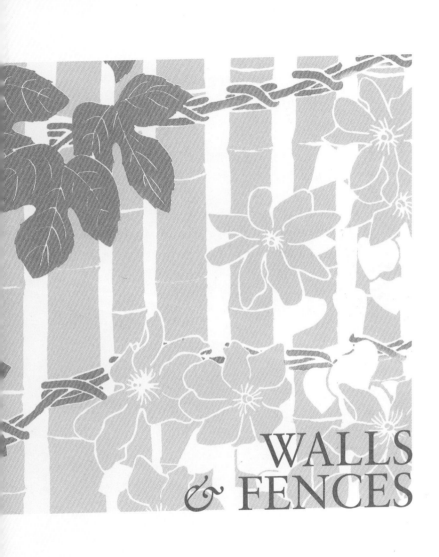

WALLS
& FENCES

Impatient Gardener's Question Time

Q *Why is my choice of fencing or walling so important?*

A Walls and fences are important to any garden but they are particularly important to the impatient gardener because they provide instant impact. In smaller gardens they are probably the most dominant element, especially in winter when there is little to distract from them. That's why it's essential to ensure that they are not merely functional but are worthwhile features in their own right.

Seven reasons why boundaries are important

1 They mark the extent of your property.

2 They provide shelter from the elements.

3 They create a warmer microclimate.

4 They provide some shade.

5 They provide an excellent backdrop to any planting scheme.

6 They provide privacy.

7 They can hide an unattractive view.

Did you know that...?

• • • densely planted walls or fences can make the boundaries of a garden disappear so that a lovely view, a nearby church spire or even the trees in neighbouring gardens appear to be part of your garden. The Japanese have a word for it – *shakkei* – meaning 'borrowed scenery'.

• • • whatever the size of your garden, internal divisions are useful because they enable you to create surprises and a sense of mystery. If the entire garden is laid out in front of you the moment you set foot in it, there's no motivation to explore and it quickly becomes predictable and boring. But when there are divisions screening parts of the garden, you're lured out to discover what's round the other side.

Impatient Gardener's Question Time

Q *I've got a long, narrow garden. How can I stop it from feeling like a tunnel?*

A The worst thing is to have a path straight down the centre and narrow borders on either side. This only emphasizes how narrow the garden is. If you divide the space up into a series of almost square, interconnecting 'rooms', it makes the space appear wider than it actually is.

Different zones, different styles

Dividing your garden into a series of 'zones' using screens or tall planting gives you the opportunity to create different garden styles in different areas. Close to the house, for example, you could have a very formal paved area with a geometric pool and clipped box topiary in pots. Beyond the first screen, you could have a cottage garden, with soft informal planting, or a Mediterranean gravel garden, or even a tropical garden. Beyond the next screen, you could have a wild area or a vegetable plot.

Screens make sense

Screens enable you to hide the less attractive elements in the garden – the tool store, the compost heap, the dustbins.

Suit the planting to the boundary

♣ Attractive old brick walls call out for traditional planting, either romantic and informal, such as herbaceous borders or the cottage-garden look, or architectural and formal, as in parterres. Smooth, rendered surfaces or painted wood suggest more modern planting with spiky architectural evergreens, grasses and perennials.

Suit the boundary to the garden

❀ Country gardens look best with informal screens such as mixed hedges – ideally, thorny ones to make them stock-proof – or on a smaller scale, wattle or willow hurdles. For the front garden, try low picket fences.

❀ City gardens need to reflect the built environment. There the best-looking boundaries are walls, smooth-planed fences, cast-iron railings or clipped formal hedges.

❀ Suburban gardens need a style somewhere between the two – neither too formal nor too informal.

Impatient Gardener's
Question Time

Q *I want to divide my garden up with some internal boundaries, but don't know what to use.*

A You don't have to worry about privacy or security where internal boundaries are concerned, so you have a wide choice. Living willow withies with their different-coloured stems make an attractive instant barrier and in summer they offer the bonus of their fresh green leaves. Plants also work – a group of shrubs, for example, or in a small garden, even one very large specimen plant. Alternatively, a section of freestanding wall not only makes a dramatic division but also provides a strong sculptural element.

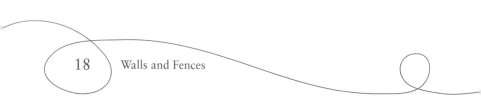

Did you know that...?

... an internal boundary doesn't necessarily have to be vertical. A change of level will also send a message that you are in a different space. Crossing water has the same effect. A rill across the garden, perhaps with a stepping stone or two, makes a very effective divide between different areas.

Two quick fixes for ugly walls

1 The easiest way to deal with ugly walls is with masonry paint. It covers a multitude of sins and brings unity to the garden at a stroke. But if your walls are in poor shape structurally, you should have them re-pointed or even rendered before you paint.

2 If the walls are beyond hope and you can't afford to tackle them right away, panels of marine plywood painted with exterior-grade paint and pinned to the walls offer an instant, low-cost, short-term solution.

Colour me beautiful

♣ When it comes to choosing colour to paint your garden walls, consider the style of your garden carefully. Soft pastels – blues, greens, lavenders – are best in a traditional garden, while crisp neutrals – greys, stone, taupe – work well in a formal setting. Stronger shades such as ochre, terracotta and plum are best in contemporary gardens. White is a good choice for a southern climate but in the north it's too harsh, especially during the grey winter months. Here, cream, soft yellow or beige are warmer choices.

* Remember that colour affects people's mood and will also affect the way you perceive the garden. 'Hot' colours such as red and orange are stimulating and energizing, and will make a garden look smaller. 'Cool' colours – blues and mauves – are relaxing and will make the space look bigger.

* You need to think, too, about the colour as a backdrop for plants. Soft blues and greens work well with everything, while stronger tones look dramatic with a 'hot' planting scheme.

Five instant tricks to liven up a dull wall

1 Use panels of trellis to break up a plain surface. They will give a 3-D effect and create attractive patterns of light and shade.

2 Parallel wooden battens of different lengths fixed to the wall also create interesting patterns and shadows. Paint them the same colour as the wall for a subtle effect, or in a contrasting colour for more drama.

3 Use stout galvanized wire to create geometric patterns – diamond shapes, zig-zags or fan shapes – on a plain surface. They add immediate interest and, in the longer term, you can grow small-leafed ivy along the wires, keeping it neatly clipped to keep the shapes sharp.

4 Screw cut-out decorative MDF panels to the wall. They come in a range of designs such as orange trees, cypresses – even Moorish windows with ornate grilles and a view beyond of minarets. To link illusion and reality, stand a palm or an orange tree in a pot in front of the panel.

5 Paint a dull brick wall with blue-green masonry paint and hang a collection of galvanized metal wall planters and watering cans on it.

Fence facelifts

The quickest and easiest way to make a difference to existing fences is with colour. Choose from wood stain, through which the grain of the wood will be visible, or specially formulated paint for external woodwork, which is opaque. Once upon a time, wood stains came in a range of 'natural' shades of brown or forest green, but the choice of colours is much wider now, with everything from subtle pastels to bold brights.

Go organic

You can find organic wood stains made from natural ingredients such as beeswax and turpentine, or you can use pigments and Danish oil to make your own.

It's a cover-up

♣ The best quick-fix solution for mis-matched fences is to cover them. The simplest option is to use split-reed or split-bamboo, which you buy in a roll and fix with staples to the fence posts. This look is really great for an oriental-style garden.

♣ For a contemporary garden, use plain panels of thin marine plywood fixed flush to the fence posts with metal brackets. You can then stain or paint the wood in the colour of your choice.

♣ For a more formal, architectural look, fix beading to the panels before you paint. Glue it on with waterproof adhesive and hammer in a few panel pins for added security. The result looks like the moulding on doors and cupboards.

Two-tone fences

You can use more than one colour to paint your fences, but do so judiciously. For instance, you could paint the posts and top rail in one colour and the panels another or paint alternate slats in different colours to give the fence 'rhythm'. Lighter and darker tones of the same shade give a subtle effect, but use a contrast if you dare.

Oriental fantasy

Try using lacquer-red posts and black panels to make a fence in a Chinese-style courtyard garden.

Finishing touches

It's remarkable what a difference you can make simply by adding finials to your fence posts. Look out for wooden balls, acorns or pyramids to transform your purely utilitarian posts into architectural features in their own right.

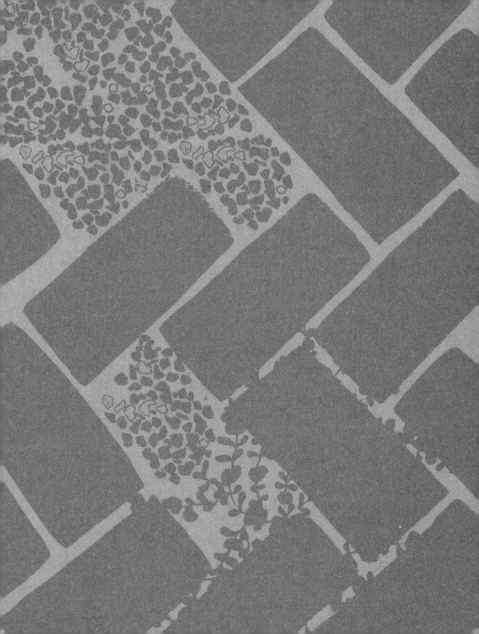

Impatient Gardener's Question Time

Q *I fancy brick walls for my garden but there are so many to choose from. Where do I start?*

A The best place to start is with your house. Ideally the bricks should match your house bricks as closely as possible. If you live in an older property, consider using second-hand bricks. They are not cheaper than new ones, but they have a lovely weathered quality and will blend with the house very quickly.

Concrete creations

Concrete is brilliant for garden walls. It can be poured into a mould and coloured, either with pigment mixed into the cement or by being painted with masonry paint after it has set. It can also be given texture by the wood used for the shuttering.

The wave effect

While boundary walls need to be straight,
there is no reason why internal concrete
walls can't be curved or even wavy.

Three quick tricks for new fencing

1 For an interesting textured look, try the 'hit and miss' style of fencing – with alternate fence poles either side of the arris rails. Leave the bark on the poles for a chunky feel, or strip then paint or stain the poles for a more formal look.

2 Cut the tops of your fence poles into points, like a stockade, or round them off for a softer, less aggressive, look.

3 Cut the fence poles all to the same length, or go for a wave formation or for castellations.

Bamboo variety

Bamboo makes a light-looking boundary that works well in both rural and urban settings. Use either stout bamboo canes, palisade style; narrower canes, split and wired together and braced at the back for support; or even a grid of canes, trellis fashion, tied together with non-perishable twine or even with thin strips of leather tied in ornamental knots.

East meets west

Add interest to a small garden without making it feel smaller by dividing it with a screen of bamboo poles and rope.

FOR A 3M (10FT) SCREEN

21 x bamboo poles approx. 10cm (4in) in diameter

35m (38yd) polypropylene rope that resembles hemp

21 x 2.5cm x 2.5cm (1 x 1in) pointed wooden stakes

60cm (2ft) long pieces of wood to act as wedges

1 Cut the bamboo poles to different lengths, ranging from 90cm (3ft) to 1.5m (5ft).

2 Hammer the pointed wooden stakes into the ground where you want each bamboo pole to be. Space them about the same distance apart as the diameter of the bamboo poles.

3 Break through the thin internal membrane of the bamboo at each nodule so the bamboo will slide easily over the stake.

4 Slot a bamboo pole over each stake, arranging them to create a graceful curve at the top. They will wobble at first, but once they are tied together, they will be stable.

5 Wedge pieces of wood between the poles to keep them vertical and to ensure the correct tension as you tie the rope.

6 Link the poles at top and bottom with the rope, making a knot at each pole. The knots can be as simple or as ornate as you like.

7 Follow the curve of the screen with your rope and knots to achieve the best effect.

Up close and personal

In town gardens, close-boarded fences are the usual choice. They are available with the planks running either horizontally or vertically. Close-fitting hardwood planks laid horizontally have a contemporary feel and make the space feel wider. For a more informal look, leave the planks uneven. Vertical planks can be either slightly overlapping – 'feathered' – or flush.

Contemporary choice

For fences in a contemporary garden, try using square panels made from planks on the diagonal. These create a bold zig-zag pattern along the boundaries. Since they are so strong visually, they work best in a rather minimalist setting. For the most stylish effect, use paint rather than stain.

Trellis works

Trellis works well in every style of garden.

* It is available in many patterns.

* It can look crisp and modern or warm and traditional.

* You can use stout trellis to make a useful screen within the garden as well as on the boundary.

* It is especially good for small spaces because it doesn't close you in too much.

* Even before any plants start growing up it, trellis creates that all-important sense of privacy.

AT GROUND LEVEL

Impatient Gardener's Question Time

Q *How does what I put at ground level in my garden help me when I'm so impatient?*

A All garden floors are ideal for an impatient gardener because they make a huge difference to the garden right away.

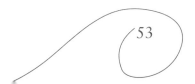

Impatient Gardener's Question Time

Q *Supposing I like a number of different ground-level treatments?*

A Most gardens have room for more than one type of surface so you can have some variety. In a garden that is largely lawn and borders, there will be at least one terrace or patio as well as paths so you can move around the garden in all weathers. And in a city garden there may be room for some slabs or decking as well as some ground-cover planting.

Two reasons to choose hard landscaping instead of lawn

1 Small areas of lawn are not practical for family gardens because they take so much wear and tear that they never look good. The inevitable bare patches will end up muddy in winter and baked hard in summer.

2 If you have a lot of shade or large trees that suck all the moisture and nutrients out of the soil, a decent-looking lawn is simply not a realistic option. Hard landscaping is the best alternative.

Did you know that...?

• • • a mixture of hard landscaping and planting is an attractive option. It's also practical because there will be areas you can use when a lawn would still be soggy after rain and, provided you choose plants that are easy to care for, it will be much less demanding in terms of maintenance than soft landscaping on its own.

Inside out

If your house or conservatory opens out onto the garden, consider carrying the same material through to give the house and garden a sense of unity. Limestone, granite, slate or large terracotta tiles are good options. The tiles will give the garden an instant Mediterranean feel – but make sure that you use frost-proof tiles outside.

All decked out

🍀 Decking works very well in many situations, ranging from inner-city backyards to rural locations.

🍀 Decking blends well with garden planting.

🍀 Decking can be cut to fit even the most awkwardly shaped areas.

🍀 If left to weather, the wood becomes a lovely soft silvery grey and looks old and rustic.

🍀 If it's colour-stained, it has a smart contemporary appearance.

Impatient Gardener's Question Time

Q *My garden slopes away from the house but I want somewhere to sit that's level. What are my options?*

A Decking is an excellent choice when you have big differences in level to contend with. In your sort of garden, it would be expensive and time-consuming to terrace the site in order to create a flat area at the top for sitting out, but it's relatively straightforward to construct a wooden deck at the top of the garden. This can be supported on stout square posts and accessed by a flight of steps. With the addition of a simple balustrade for safety, the deck will provide not just a useful seating area but also a great view.

Impatient Gardener's Question Time

Q *I've got an old, cracked concrete patio and I want to cover it quickly. Any ideas?*

A Decking is a great choice to lay over existing surfaces. You don't have to dig out the concrete first, nor do you have to consider those boring but essential details such as the level of the house's damp-proof course. Since air circulates freely through and under decking, it doesn't matter if the decking finishes above the damp-proof course.

Three decking choices

1 Hardwoods such as teak and oak are very expensive but will last a lifetime. Pressure-treated softwoods are less expensive but can also last many years.

2 Consider using recycled timber – old floorboards or even dismantled pallets. Left untreated, the aged appearance of old floorboards is part of their charm, while recycled pallets can be stained so the wood is indistinguishable from new.

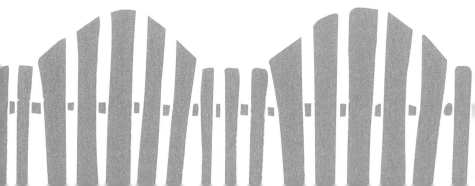

3 Choose between grooved and smooth decking. Some people think grooved decking is better on the grounds that it is less slippery when wet, but in fact the grooves fill with soil and debris unless the decking is swept regularly, so you can end up with a smooth surface anyway. At the end of the day, it's down to personal choice.

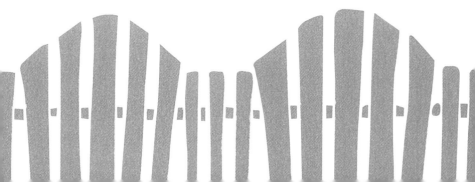

A suitable case for treatment

Softwood that has not been pressure-treated needs to be specially treated to prolong its life. Either use a clear preservative every few years or coloured wood stain, some types of which are specially formulated for decking.

Colour effects

If you choose to use a wood stain on your decking, there is a good range of colours, from subtle silver greys to natural browns and more vibrant blues and yellows. But think carefully about your choice because a large area of strongly coloured flooring will have enormous visual impact, especially during the winter.

Impatient Gardener's Question Time

Q *Help! I've inherited an entire small garden made up of dirty, stained, concrete slabs. I don't want to keep them long term, but I can't afford to replace them right away. What can I do?*

A For a temporary improvement, use paint. It won't last indefinitely, but it will make a big difference. Start by cleaning the slabs with a proprietary patio and path cleaner or a pressure washer. Then paint them with step and tile paint. Technically, this isn't recommended for outside use, but I know it will last long enough to do the job you want it to do. Masonry paint is another option. Though it's fine for outside use, it isn't recommended for floors either; but again, I know that it works well. And it comes in a much wider range of colours than step and tile paint, so offers more scope for artistic flair.

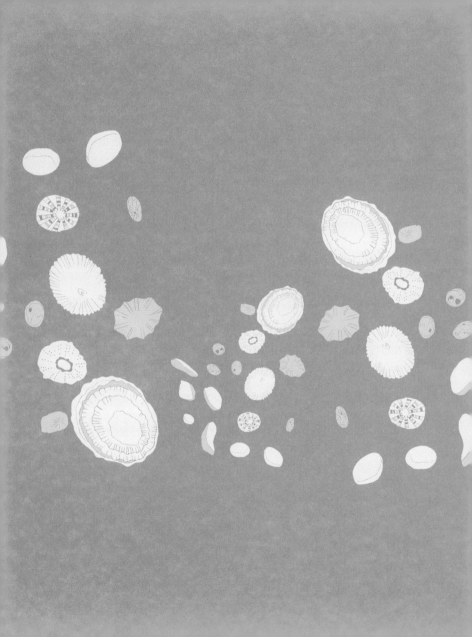

Impatient Gardener's
Question Time

Q *I'd love to decorate my old slab floor with paint but I'm not very artistic. Is there anything I can do instead?*

A If you only want a small painted design, you could try using a stencil, either bought from a craft shop or – if you're feeling adventurous – home made. Simple geometric shapes such as circles, ovals and diamonds work best and are simple to use.

New life for tired slabs

A startling pattern of blue and orange circles can't fail to liven up an area of old slabs. Apply the design as a border or an all-over random pattern. As a finishing touch, spray a simple terracotta bowl with copper acrylic all-surface aerosol paint and plant with several *Echeveria elegans*. These have fleshy blue leaves and tall slender sprays of bright orange flowers that complement the paint colours very well. Echeverias are not hardy, so bring them inside in winter where they make attractive houseplants.

YOU WILL NEED:
- stiff corrugated cardboard

- 1 x can blue multi-surface aerosol garden paint

- 1 x can orange multi-surface aerosol garden paint

1 Cut a piece of cardboard the same size as a slab. Cut a large circle out of the rectangle and a small circle out of the large circle.

2 Place the template in position on a slab and remove the large circle, leaving the small circle and the outer section in place.

3 Spray the slab using the blue paint.

4 When this is dry, replace the large circle, remove the small one and spray with orange paint.

5 Repeat as necessary.

Patio paving facelifts

❀ Try replacing a few of your patio slabs – perhaps some damaged ones if there are any – with a new, contrasting material as in the suggestions opposite.

❀ Use brick pavers laid in a herringbone pattern, forming a series of 'V's or in a basket-weave design, with two pavers laid lengthways, two widthways, and so on.

❀ Use closely packed cobbles laid end on or side on.

❀ Use old roofing tiles or slates. Cut them in half and lay them side on in a zig-zag or sunray pattern.

❀ Try a mosaic made from small coloured pebbles or even seashells set in cement. Work out your pattern on paper first and make sure the mosaic is flush with the surrounding paving by pressing lightly down on the mosaic with a plank as you work.

❀ Steel and brass washers in a variety of sizes look very stylish, especially if laid at random and overlapping.

❀ Use glass marbles or iridescent glass florists' nuggets set in white cement rather than the usual grey. This will give a light, bright background and show off the colours at their dazzling best.

Act natural

* If you're planning on a new floor surface for the garden, natural stone is superb. Whether it's old and weathered or newly cut, it comes in a beautifully subtle range of colours from almost pure white to black, taking in everything from pinks, beiges, browns, purples and greys en route. It is also extremely hardwearing and, unlike so many other materials, only gets better with age.

* Slate, granite, sandstone and carboniferous limestone (oölitic limestone is probably too soft for outside use) are all good choices. If you live in an area that has its own local stone, it makes sense to use it, not least because it will help keep costs down.

Impatient Gardener's
Question Time

Q *I love the look of stone but can't afford it as the area I want to pave is pretty big. Is there an alternative?*

A Not long ago, reproduction stone slabs were a poor imitation of the real thing, but now they're greatly improved, especially the ones made of reconstituted ground natural stone. They are made in moulds based on natural stone slabs so the surface texture is very realistic indeed.

Colour matters

✿ Before you commit yourself to a choice
of stone slabs, look at them wet as well
as dry because the colour can change
quite dramatically – and in temperate
climates you'll be seeing them wet a lot
of the time.

✿ It's also best to stick to one colour.
Those chequerboard patios and paths
in pink and yellow slabs that were so
popular in the 1970s and 1980s really
do look like rhubarb and custard.

Dressed or undressed?

Dressed slabs have a smooth, sometimes almost polished, finish and perfectly straight edges so they work best in formal or modern gardens. Undressed slabs, which have a riven, textured surface and irregular edges, work best in an informal setting. Here use slabs of different sizes, leave the edges unaligned and the joints unpointed. You could fill any gaps with soil mixed with seeds such as Erigeron, Alyssum, or California poppies (*Eschscholzia*) – or wait for moss to colonize them.

Crazy or what?

Crazy paving is another option for an informal garden. Buying off-cuts of stone is a less expensive means of using real stone, but even broken reproduction slabs can look good if they are well laid, with a generous amount of mortar between the pieces and perhaps framed with lines of brick to create geometric panels.

Size and scale

♣ One school of thought says that it's best to use the largest possible size of slabs in a small area because that results in fewer joints. This will make the space will look less 'busy' and so it will feel larger. The other view is that where space is limited, very large units look out of proportion and this will make the area appear even smaller, while more compact units, especially if laid in a simple unfussy pattern, can make the space feel larger.

✽ Small units are easier to lay as they need less cutting to make them fit. If you are doing the work yourself, base your layout on the dimensions of your materials to avoid having to cut at all. Also, if your design involves curves or circles, small units are much easier to work with than larger ones.

Just add plants

You can add interest to an existing patio by removing some whole slabs and planting in the spaces. On a small patio though, large areas of planting can look out of proportion. In this case, remove just part of a slab.

Four evergreen carpeters to add interest to hard surfaces

1 Carpeting thymes are good value. They offer winter interest, have small pink, mauve, red or white flowers in early summer, and release their fragrance when they are stepped on.

2 Thrift (*Armeria maritima*) is another good choice, forming soft hummocks of long, slender, bright evergreen leaves and with masses of bright pink clover-like flowers in summer.

3 The New Zealand burr (*Acaena microphylla* 'Copper Carpet' syn. *A. m.* 'Kupferteppich'), which forms a carpet of tiny coppery leaves with small, round, spiky flowers of chestnut brown, looks especially good with yellow bricks or setts.

4 *Stachys byzantina* 'Silver Carpet' is grown for its attractive furry silver leaves, not its flowers, so this non-flowering variety is particularly welcome. It makes an attractive ground-cover plant in very free-draining, gritty soil and full sun.

A concrete idea

✿ Poured concrete is adored by many modern garden designers as a flooring material. It can be used to make any shape you like and can be tinted to produce a range of subtle or bold colours. It works best when it is unashamedly itself and not moulded to mimic setts, cobbles or pavers.

✿ Although any competent home handyperson or builder can lay concrete successfully, to exploit the design potential of the material fully, it is best to use a specialist company.

Go for brick...

❧ Match the bricks you use for garden paving as closely as possible to those of the house, though the house bricks themselves may not be ideal. Used on the ground, house bricks may absorb water, which expands as it freezes and contracts as it thaws. The result? Crumbly bricks. Instead, make sure you use frost-proof bricks. The hardest bricks of all are non-porous engineering bricks, which are often blue-black. These look very striking in a formal or modern garden.

❀ Brick comes in a number of different colours from dark blue-black, through a variety of shades of red and brown to deep yellow ochre and even cream.

...or try pavers

❀ Pavers, which have roughly the same visible dimensions as bricks when laid but are about half the thickness, are specially made for paving.

A sense of direction

Laid lengthways, bricks or pavers add forward movement to a path or patio, leading the eye off into the distance. Laid widthways, they draw the eye out to the sides, emphasizing the width rather than the length and so making the whole space feel wider. Patterns such as basket-weave are static; in other words, they do not lead the eye in any particular direction, and so are more suitable for patios and other sitting areas.

Get sett

Setts are square (10cm/4in) blocks of granite, real or imitation, with a slightly rounded upper face. They are good for making intricate flooring patterns and for tight curves and circles. The curved tops give an interesting textured surface. Use them on their own, as decoration to break up an area of slabs or as an edging to contain gravel.

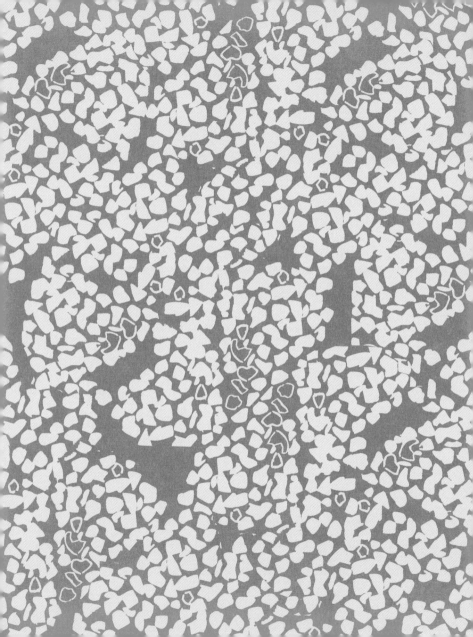

Six reasons to make gravel your choice

1 Gravel can have an informal or Mediterranean feel about it or it can be formal, used with low clipped hedges to create a parterre effect.

2 It is an ideal material for integrating the hard and soft elements within a garden because you can grow plants through and even in it.

3 It's inexpensive.

4 It can be used for drives, parking areas, paths and patios, as long as they have firm foundations.

5 It can be used to great effect in combination with other hard materials such as York stone, bricks, setts and cobbles.

6 It may just be spread loose in borders to bring a uniform look to an area.

Did you know that...?

... gravel and chippings are available in a wide range of colours, the colours varying depending on the area they come from. If you don't live in an area that produces its own gravel, choose a colour range that blends with your house or with the other hard materials in the garden. York stone, for example, looks best with cool grey gravel, while yellow sandstone looks good with warm golden gravel.

Size matters

♣ Gravel comes in different sizes, from very fine to chunky. A medium grade is most practical because it doesn't stick to your shoes and get walked into the house so easily. Also, cats find the stones too large and heavy to scratch in.

♣ If you are covering a slight slope, angular gravel is better than smooth, round pea gravel. The stones grip together and don't move as much.

Ouch!

For pedestrian traffic, gravel should be
at most 2.5cm (1in) deep, otherwise it is
uncomfortable to walk on and will ridge
up. So either lay it on a firm foundation
or use a weed-suppressing membrane
underneath and stepping stones of another
material as a path through it.

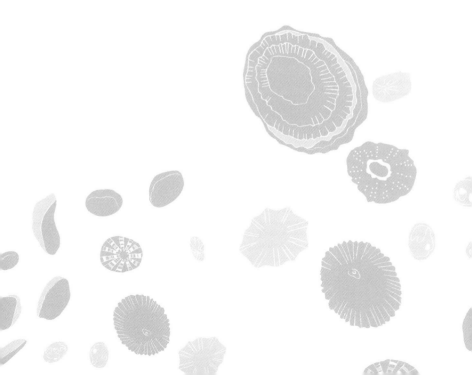

Impatient Gardener's Question Time

Q *What will give me a similar look to gravel but with a more cutting-edge feel?*

A Crushed glass, which is laid in the same way as gravel, is a very stylish, though more expensive option. It comes in a range of bright colours such as violet and turquoise. It has been tumbled to remove all sharp edges, so it is perfectly safe. Smooth oval florists' beads are another option, but they are more expensive in large quantities.

Another very smart alternative is fine aluminium or stainless-steel chippings or granules. You can even use crushed CDs.

Impatient Gardener's Question Time

Q *I like the look of these materials but don't fancy having them distributed all over the garden by people or animals walking on them. Is there a solution?*

A Many of the finer grades can be bonded to a resinated base. This gives the same appearance but without the disadvantages.

Four reasons to choose grass

1 In the form of turf, which can be laid instantly like carpet, rather than seed, which takes some weeks to grow, grass is well suited to the needs of the impatient gardener.

2 Grass works very well in traditional settings and there is no doubt that a sward of perfect emerald green sets plants off beautifully.

3 It's the obvious choice for medium and large gardens, both rural and urban, where hard landscaping would be both inappropriate and financially ruinous.

4 It's also the surface best suited to family gardens – provided the area of lawn is large enough – as it provides somewhere for children to play.

Turf special

* Turf looks good the instant it is laid – great for impatient gardeners – but it will still be a few weeks before it has rooted into the soil, is growing strongly and can be walked on.

* Choose the grade of turf that is most suitable for the way you plan to use the lawn. Very fine grade looks best, though it needs a lot of upkeep. A tougher grade will take more punishment but won't look quite so plush. For a shady garden, choose a shade-tolerant grade.

* Turf is best laid in autumn when there is still some warmth in the soil but there is likely to be plenty of rain, or in early spring, as the soil begins to warm up and there is also likely to be plenty of rain. You can lay it in summer, but then you will need to make sure it is watered regularly, or the joins may open up and ugly gaps appear.

Mowing made easy

Set stepping stones or paving just below the level of the grass so that the mower can skim over the whole lot, removing the need for time-consuming edge-trimming. Bricks or pavers can also form a useful barrier between lawn and border plants, which may be inclined to flop over it and kill off the grass underneath. If you like the look of irregular slabs of York stone adjoining a lawn, be prepared to keep the edges trimmed with scissors!

The grass alternative

🍀 Chamomile and thyme are often suggested as alternatives to grass but in large spaces they are a considerable amount of work in the early stages. In small areas, though, surrounded by hard materials, they are easier to maintain. Neither plant minds being trodden on occasionally, and indeed, when crushed, they release their fragrance, but they would not make a suitable surface for family picnics or energetic games.

🍀 Corsican mint is another alternative, especially in shade. It has minute pale mauve flowers and very small round green leaves that smell powerfully of peppermint when touched or walked on.

CONTAINERS

Two reasons to choose containers

1 If you have nothing more than a courtyard garden, balcony, roof terrace or basement area, containers are the only place you can grow plants.

2 If you have a proper garden, containers are a way of adding instant, eye-distracting beauty either on the patio, or even placed among dull neglected shrubs in a border – perfect for impatient gardeners.

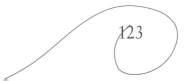

Impatient Gardener's Question Time

Q *I'm really short of time. Can I have containers that look good all year round without spending every weekend planting them and caring for them?*

A Easy. You can plant a container for a display that lasts most of the year – bulbs for spring and bedding for summer and winter. Choose small varieties of bulbs so that once flowering is over, the dying foliage is not too prominent. Or you can grow plants for a short spectacular season – Regale lilies perhaps, for their breathtaking fragrance in mid-summer, or a dazzling deciduous azalea in spring. Once they have finished their show, simply move them to a less prominent position, then bring them out again next year.

Did you know that...?

... If you're constantly moving home, containers are a good choice because you can take them with you when you go. You may be reluctant to spend a lot of money on a specimen tree to plant in the garden because you only plan to stay a year or two, but plant it in a suitably large container and you can take it with you. When you do finally settle down, simply plant the tree in the garden.

• • • containers are great for plants that may need some protection in winter – spiky exotic Agaves and Aeoniums, or half-hardy perennials such as Pelargoniums, Argyranthemums and Osteospermums. If there is no room for them inside over the winter, group them together in a sheltered corner of the garden and cover them with sacking or bubble wrap.

Impatient Gardener's
Question Time

Q *I've never done any gardening before.*
What sort of plants can I grow in a container?

A Almost anything, from a tree to a lettuce.
Many small trees do well, for example Japanese
maples, rowans, whitebeams, crab apples and
flowering cherries. You can also grow apples
and cherries along with peaches and apricots.
And that's not to mention a whole range of
shrubs, particularly evergreens and roses – patio
varieties, ground-cover, English roses and
climbing roses. Then there are perennials such as
hostas, ferns and many grasses, also annuals and
bulbs, especially the spring-flowering kind. The
list is endless.

Just add water

You can even plant aquatic plants in your container. Use a large pot without a drainage hole, fill it between half and two-thirds full of soil or special aquatic compost, add a little carbon to prevent the soil becoming sour and the water stagnant, then put in your plant. Finally, fill the pot with water. A pot like this is ideal if you go away a lot because it can be left for several weeks without needing to be topped up with water.

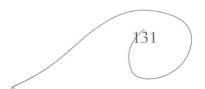

Impatient Gardener's Question Time

Q *I've heard that some plants can be fussy about the soil they grow in. Is this true and if so what can I do if my garden's got the wrong sort of soil?*

A Go for containers. Acid-lovers such as rhododendrons and camellias need lime-free soil. If you do not have this in the garden, just plant them in containers. Equally, some Mediterranean plants such as rosemary and lavender hate heavy boggy soil, so grow them in pots in a free-draining gritty compost.

Containers

Eat me

Edible crops such as herbs and salads –
especially cut-and-come-again salad leaves
– do well in containers and small, specially
bred tomatoes can be grown either in a
pot or a hanging basket, along with some
pale blue trailing lobelia – an attractive
and unusual combination. Look out for
specially bred sweet peppers, aubergines
and chillies for patio containers too.

Big is beautiful

Whatever container you choose, always go for the largest you can afford. Not only does one big one have greater impact than several smaller ones, but it is also more practical because the compost will dry out less quickly and so need less watering.

Two designer tips

1 If you do want several containers, they will make more of a show if they are all the same style and material and are grouped together rather than dotted about.

2 If you have a large, particularly striking container, you could just leave it unplanted and have it make a strong sculptural statement among the planting in a border or on a patio.

What's inside?

♣ All containers need adequate drainage holes and a layer of drainage material to prevent the compost washing into the holes. Traditionally 'crocks' – broken pieces of terracotta flowerpot – are used but you can use large pebbles or broken slates or tiles. Where weight is a consideration, polystyrene packaging broken into manageable pieces is ideal.

♣ For permanent plantings, choose a soil-based compost such as John Innes No. 3, while for temporary annual plantings, a soil-less compost is fine. For permanent plantings on a roof or balcony where weight is a consideration, use a mixture of the two.

Material girl

♣ There is a huge range of ceramic pots for the garden in all shapes and sizes, ranging from Chinese cloud pots in rich dark blue or turquoise, hand-decorated pots from Mediterranean countries, dainty pots that look great as a table centrepiece or wall-hanging pots with flat backs. Just make sure the pot's frost-proof before you buy.

♣ Wood in the form of half-barrels or square rough-sawn tubs suits informal, romantic gardens. Alternatively, choose painted square Versailles tubs, with panelled sides and knobs at each corner for a formal setting.

♣ There are some very good wood imitation containers made of plastic or fibreglass that need little looking after. The best are made from moulds of the genuine article so the wood grain looks extremely convincing even close up.

✤ Square or rectangular lead tanks work well in a traditional setting, although the reproduction versions made from fibreglass are totally convincing, much lighter in weight and carry no health risk. Other metals such as copper, aluminium, stainless steel and galvanized metal in strong, simple geometric shapes, look very good in a modern formal garden.

✤ Glass containers need to be thick and toughened. Try it for growing plants such as the tall papyrus (*Cyperus papyrus*) hydroponically, in layers of coloured gravel or bright plastic chippings and water. If you want to grow plants in the normal way in glass, you will need drainage holes in the bottom of the container – get a professional to make them for you.

♣ Baskets woven from willow make terrific containers if you treat them with several coats of coloured wood stain or waterproof yacht varnish first and line them with stout black polythene before you plant. They will not last forever but will give you a lot of container for your money for a few years.

♣ Large stone urns look marvellous in large gardens – evoking the great classical gardens of Italy and France – but they can also be stunning in very small city gardens where their disproportionate scale is very dramatic and exciting.

❋ Genuine antique stone containers can cost as much as a second-hand car, but reproduction urns of reconstituted stone are cheaper, and concrete replicas are cheapest of all. These do look rather stark and new but can easily be 'distressed' with a hammer and chisel, and a coat of well-watered-down dark brown emulsion to age them. If you can curb your impatience just this once, painting them with plain yoghurt or sour milk, or even liquid manure, quickly encourages algae and lichen to grow on them, adding a welcome patina of age.

Terracotta tradition

♣ Terracotta containers work well in almost all gardens but are particularly good in an informal or romantic setting. They are available in a range of styles, from plain machine-made flowerpots to highly decorated hand-thrown pots. Your choice will be dictated by taste and budget but, especially if you are buying expensive terracotta, make sure it is guaranteed frost-proof.

♣ A row of terracotta half-pots filled with lavender have a soft, traditional feel while still looking formal.

Not quite terracotta

♣ Very good plastic imitation terracotta pots look almost like the real thing. They have the advantage of being lightweight and unbreakable, although they do not age in the same way.

♣ They can look extremely stylish with a paint effect. Try an easy-to-use kit for a verdigris, pewter or rusty-iron look. Always use an acrylic undercoat and seal with waterproof varnish.

Simple or ornate?

The more elaborate the container, the simpler the display of plants in it needs to be and vice versa. So a very ornately decorated pot will look stunning with just one type of plant – for instance trailing scarlet pelargoniums or blue-leafed hostas – while a plain wooden half-barrel needs a more interesting combination of shapes and colours.

Pack them in

The most attractive containers are those
that are packed with plants. You don't
want to see any bare compost and, in the
case of a simple container, you don't want
to see a great deal of the container, either.

Ups and downs

Choose plants of different habits – some
trailing to soften the edges, some upright to
add height to the display and some bushy
to fill in.

Impatient Gardener's Question Time

Q *I haven't got a clue about colour schemes for my container planting. Can you help?*

A A limited range of colours works best. Red, white and blue is always popular with traditional gardeners, while for a romantic garden, pastels such as pink, mauve, pale blue and white together with silver foliage look terrific. Single-colour planting can look stunning too. Yellow, for example, ranges from deep cream through lemon, butter and apricot to deep gold. White is always very elegant. Here the interest comes from the contrasting flower shapes and sizes, together with the different greens of the foliage. Try tiny white lobelia or gypsophila, with larger busy lizzies and big blowsy double begonias.

Perfect positioning

In a formal garden, part of what makes
the difference to your containers is where
you position them. A pair of identical
containers either side of a front door or
a bench, for example, immediately adds
a sense of formality, or try four matching
containers at the corners of a square or
rectangular pool.

Did you know that...?

... architectural plants – those with very large boldly shaped leaves – are ideally suited to formality because they reinforce the simple geometry of the containers themselves. Spiky evergreen cordylines, phormiums or large-leafed hostas are all very good choices.

Two topiary tales

1 Topiary – small-leafed evergreen shrubs such as box, euonymus or holly clipped into geometric shapes – is an excellent choice for container planting. All an impatient gardener needs is a single box ball or lollipop, spiral or pyramid to make an immediate impact.

2 Box topiary takes careful training over a number of years, so it's an expensive buy. As a less expensive alternative, stand a trellis or wire obelisk in your container. This will create that sharp architectural outline right away, then you can grow a fast-growing plant such as a small-leafed plain green ivy over it. If you keep it well clipped, the outline will remain crisp and the angles sharp.

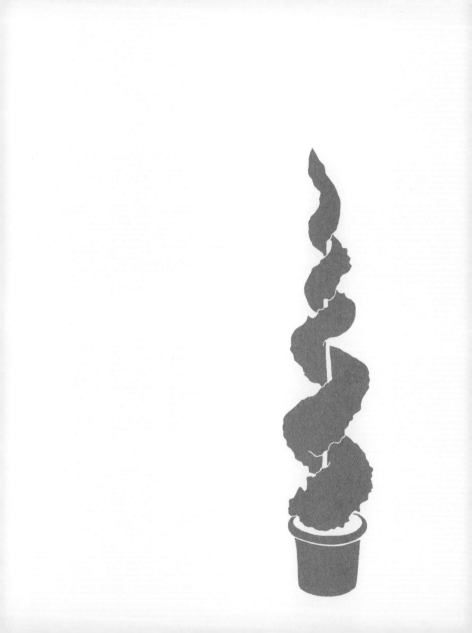

Herbal chequerboard

This herb garden is perfect for the impatient gardener who also loves to cook because it can be used – judiciously – from day one. Your choice of herbs depends on what you most like to use and what will suit the conditions best. For example, mint likes some shade, while Mediterranean herbs such as thyme and rosemary need sun. And since this herb garden should be decorative as well as functional, choose herbs that look, as well as taste, good.

YOU WILL NEED
5 x square metal containers
30 x 30 x 30cm (12 x 12 x 12in)

approximately 4.5m (15ft)
of 5 x 2.5cm (2 x 1in) timber

4 x 'L' brackets

black gloss paint for exterior use

1 x 2-litre (3½-pint) pot
Rosmarinus 'Miss Jessopp's Upright'

4 x 9-cm (3½-in) pots *Salvia officinalis* 'Purpurascens'

4 x 9-cm (3½-in) pots mint

4 x 9-cm (3½-in) pots chives

4 x 9-cm (3½-in) pots *Foeniculum vulgare* 'Purpureum'

4 x 9-cm (3½-in) pots thyme

soil-based compost

decorative mulch of crushed CDs

1 Arrange the 5 metal containers in a chequerboard pattern.

2 Make a frame of 5 x 2.5cm (2 x 1in) timber, joined at the corners with simple metal 'L' brackets and large enough to surround the containers.

3 Paint the frame black and put it in position.

4 Fill the containers almost to the top with the compost and plant one with rosemary, one with purple sage, one with mint, one with chives and one with bronze fennel – or with herbs of your own choice.

LIGHTING

Impatient Gardener's
Question Time

Q *I may be an impatient gardener but I'm not a millionaire. Why on earth should I bother with any garden lighting? Isn't it just another unnecessary expense?*

A There are so many advantages to garden lighting it's difficult to know where to begin. For a start, it enables you to enjoy all the other features in your garden, whether you are sitting outside or looking at the garden from indoors. And if you go out to work, you probably have little opportunity to enjoy your garden because it's so often dark by the time you get home. The use of lighting can change all that.

In fact, your garden may look even better at night because you can highlight the very best bits and hide the less good ones under a forgiving cloak of darkness – especially important if you are an impatient gardener who has only improved one area of the garden so far.

And finally, since you're so impatient, remember that lighting gives you instant drama at the flick of a switch.

Did you know that...?

... lighting can be as simple or as complicated as you like. Choose from simple candles or lanterns or go for electric lights – either low-voltage systems you can install yourself or more sophisticated lighting that needs to be installed by a professional.

The simplest of simple lighting effects for a special occasion

🍀 Drape strings of low-voltage outdoor lights over the branches of trees or shrubs or over statues or obelisks. Choose from little round pea lights, light-emitting diodes (LEDs) in flexible plastic tubing, or fibre-optic cables. Coloured lights are fun for a party. Set them to twinkle or 'chase' each other. Most of these lighting sets come with a programmer and a number of programming options.

🍀 Hang glass and metal lanterns with tea lights inside from the branches of trees or big shrubs or put glass storm lanterns on a garden table.

* Use a mass of glass jars with a tea light in each to light a path, along the top of a wall or in a large group on the patio floor. The more you have, the more magical the effect. If you want some colour, simply paint the outside of the jam jars with translucent glass paint.

* Part-fill large stiff brown paper bags with sand for stability and add a tea light to each. They will cast a lovely warm golden glow. You can buy bags that have been specially treated with a fire-retardant.

* If you have a pool or pond, float some special floating candles in it. The slightest movement of the water makes both the real and the reflected flames dance and sparkle.

* Candles pushed into the soil in flowerpots are an instant and very inexpensive form of garden lighting.

Impatient Gardener's
Question Time

Q *Must I have a professional to install my garden lighting?*

A While you can install low-voltage DIY lighting yourself, you will need a qualified electrician for any other sort of lighting, especially lighting associated with water. And since lighting your garden is not just about the practicalities but about aesthetics too, it is worth employing a professional to design the layout. A good designer will arrive at your home with a set of lights to show you how the garden could look at night.

But whichever route you go down, if you are planning a garden from scratch, think about the lighting from the start rather than adding it as an afterthought once the garden is finished.

Degrees of separation

If you want to install sensor-triggered security lighting, it needs to be on a separate circuit.

A touch of theatre

Take your cue from theatre lighting to achieve the best lighting effects in your garden.

✿ *Front light*
Statues or particularly ornate urns or pots are best lit from the front so that the detail is revealed. If they are lit from behind, you tend to just see a silhouette.

✿ *Side light*
Side lighting is best for an object whose three-dimensional shape is its outstanding feature, such as a simple pot or an abstract sculpture.

Side lighting is ideal for illuminating steps or other changes of level.

✿ Bottom light

Trees look fantastic lit from below, their tracery of branches standing out against the darkness.

Lighting from below with uplighters is great for walls too. Around an eating area they create a soft background glow and you could add a few candles on the table so people can see what they're eating.

Uplighters can be used to mark a path if you're looking for a subtle effect.

✿ Top light

Downlighters create discrete pools of light, which is another useful way of marking features such as steps. You can either hang the fittings low enough for them to be hidden by any planting or suspend them high up in a tree where they can shine down through the branches.

What's your style?

You can use light to emphasize the style of your garden. In a formal garden, for example, narrow beams of light at regular intervals shining up a wall would add to the formality, while softer more diffuse lights set at different angles and washing over the wall would give a much more informal feel. In modern gardens, the latest technology in fibre optics, as well as neon, takes lighting into the realm of art.

Water wizardry do's and don'ts

✿ Do use uplighters underwater in a formal pool. They look especially good placed directly under a fountain or jet.

✿ Do try an underwater uplighter in a simple bubble fountain. It will steal the show.

✿ Do turn the spotlight on a wall fountain and watch each falling droplet sparkle in the light.

✿ Do try side lighting for a pool. It creates strong shadows from any planting and turns a still surface into a mirror, giving you great reflections.

✿ Don't use downlighters in a pond because they reveal all the mechanics – cables, pumps, pond liners – and of course, any debris in the water. They also create an uncomfortable glare.

Shadow play

When you're planning your lighting effects, you also need to consider the impact that shadow has. An architectural plant lit from below will cast fantastic magnified shadows on a nearby wall. In my own garden, the shadows cast by the jagged blue leaves of *Melianthus major* look like palm trees on my terracotta wall and turn a part of south-west London at night into southern California.

ARCHES
& ARBOURS

Impatient Gardener's Question Time

Q *What's the difference between an arbour, a pergola and a gazebo?*

A Traditionally, an arbour was a leafy bower of densely planted trees or shrubs trained together overhead to create a private, shady place to sit. Now, the term is more widely used for any enclosed seating area where plants, though still important, no longer form the structure.

A pergola consists of a series of uprights linked by overheads. It's rather like a walk-through 'tunnel' so you often find one standing on a path. It can also be attached to the house, making a useful visual link between house and garden.

Gazebos were primarily ornamental, adding structure to the garden or framing a statue. They are usually round or octagonal in shape, so they need to be in an open prominent position.

Arches and Arbours

Three ways of using arches

1 A simple arch divides the garden and so creates a sense of surprise, which is especially important in a small garden where the tendency is to see the whole garden the moment you step out into it.

2 Position an arch in front of a wall, grow some lovely climbers over it, place a seat underneath and hey presto! you've got a leafy arbour.

3 Line up two or three arches and you've got a pergola.

Did you know that...?

... pergolas, arches and arbours not only add height and structure to your garden but are also important to the way you use and enjoy the space, giving you a sense of being inside even though you are outside. And they also help create a feeling of privacy, which, in overcrowded cities with neighbours so close by, is invaluable.

All in the mind

🍀 While you can have an arbour that is completely enclosed with solid timber or trellis, even a light structure of poles, ropes or netting creates a haven and makes you feel safe from prying eyes.

🍀 Enclosing part of your garden with a pergola makes the spaces at either end feel more open and therefore larger.

🍀 Pergolas can suggest movement around the garden, dividing it up and yet linking different areas.

Eight pergola pointers

1 Stone or brick piers with wooden overheads were popular in nineteenth- and early twentieth-century gardens, but wood is the most common choice for the uprights these days since it is relatively inexpensive and quick to erect.

2 For a modern garden, try using an 'industrial' material such as scaffolding poles, welded square-section metal or reinforced steel joists painted with tough external-grade enamel. Lengths of copper piping or stainless-steel chain or cable can make striking overheads for a wooden pergola.

3 For a more organic look, make the overheads from stout polypropylene rope, which looks like hemp, or from lengths of bamboo.

4 In an informal garden, and especially at some distance from the house, natural-looking rustic poles have a cottage-garden feel, but close to the house, and certainly in more formal gardens, square posts are better. You can make them look even smarter by chamfering the corners and painting or staining them either a dark colour – navy or black – or a pale blue-green or grey.

5 Square, unpainted timber overheads give a solid chunky feel, while narrower timbers, arranged in a grid, are more elegant, especially if the ends of the timbers are shaped.

6 If you've got the space, consider positioning a pergola at a point where two paths cross.

7 In a very small garden, it's best to attach a pergola to the house or to a side wall rather than have it freestanding, where it will take up a lot of space.

8 Your pergola – or any garden arch for that matter – must be tall and wide enough for people to walk under and through, even when it is clothed with plants.

Did you know that…?

… an arbour is perfect for the impatient gardener as it's very striking visually and has instant impact.

An open and shut case

🌸 Some arbours are made of solid timber, rather like sentry boxes. They can be rectangular or arched, plain or fancy, double or single, and some have a built-in seat.

🌸 Other arbours are made from trellis panels, with the degree of enclosure they offer depending on the spaces between the battens.

Traditional...?

Woven willow or hazel makes an attractive arbour. Hazel works better in an informal garden because it's rather chunkier-looking, while willow makes very clean shapes that are good in a formal setting. You can leave the twigs unpainted or give them a wash of colour – pale grey or even white looks very stylish.

...or modern?

Unashamedly modern materials such as polycarbonate panels, especially used in conjunction with steel uprights, make a striking contemporary arbour. It will be well sheltered from the wind, private and yet filled with light.

Men in sheds

Sheds are functional, but that doesn't mean they have to be ugly. Rather than hide them behind a screen, paint them an attractive colour to make a statement – beach-hut blue-and-white stripes in a gravel garden, for example, or rich Harrods green with gold fittings.

Summerhouse special

- Summerhouses may sound rather grand, but it is possible to find them at a size and price suitable for most gardens, and they not only add weight to the overall design of the garden, but also provide a sheltered place to sit, even on days that are bright but cold.

- If you want your summerhouse to blend in, paint it the same colour or perhaps a shade darker or lighter than the surrounding greenery or boundaries. If you want to make it a focal point, use a contrasting shade.

FURNITURE

Impatient Gardener's Question Time

Q *What's the quickest – and cheapest – thing I can do to stop my overgrown garden from looking neglected?*

A Just buy a good-looking garden chair – even a simple, coloured, plastic folding chair will do – and pop it in the garden in a spot that catches the sun. It will make an instant focal point, no-one will notice the wildness around it, and you'll have somewhere great to sit as well.

Shopping advisor

♣ Seats must be comfortable and tables sturdy.

♣ Tables and chairs must be easily moved and stored if they are not weatherproof.

♣ In very small gardens, particularly, tables and chairs have to look good because they will be a very prominent part of the scene.

♣ If you want wooden furniture, choose from hard- or softwood. Hardwood can stay outside in winter and will last for many years. If you oil it regularly, it will keep its glossy brown colour, otherwise it will weather to a silvery grey. Pressure-treated softwood is less expensive and won't last quite as long, though regular treatment with coloured woodstain or opaque paint will prolong its life.

- Curved wood furniture is expensive as the curves are achieved by complicated lamination and steaming.

- Reproduction cast-aluminium tables and chairs are lightweight and don't need much maintenance.

- Seats moulded from polypropylene in bold free-form shapes and bright colours are surprisingly comfortable and very sculptural when not in use.

- Plastic garden furniture is the cheapest. If that's all your budget runs to, you can always brighten it up by treating it with an acrylic undercoat and spraying it an interesting colour with plastic spray paint.

One style suits all

Simple café-style tables and chairs work in almost every style of garden. Plain aluminium or bright, funky lime-green, orange or blue make a youthful statement. Off-white, pastels and dark green have a more classic appeal.

In with the new

Wooden furniture for modern gardens
should have simple clean lines, whether
angular or curved.

In with the old

Traditional Lutyens or Chinese
Chippendale benches work well with tables
and chairs in strong geometric shapes.

Old to new

A random collection of old kitchen chairs
takes on a more unified look when painted
all the same colour or in complementary
shades. They won't be weatherproof
though, so remember not to leave them out
in the garden.

Sun worshipper

Look for the corner of the garden that catches the last rays of the sun and put some seating there.

Spaced out

If storage space is a problem, buy folding garden chairs in bright colours and hang them on the garden walls. Instant art!

WATER

Three good reasons to have a water feature in the garden

1 It brings a sense of movement to the garden. Even a still water feature does this in the form of ripples across the surface and reflections of clouds and of plants moving in the wind.

2 The sound of water is wonderfully relaxing, especially in busy towns and cities.

3 Water attracts a whole range of wildlife – birds, frogs, newts, dragonflies – often within days, if not hours.

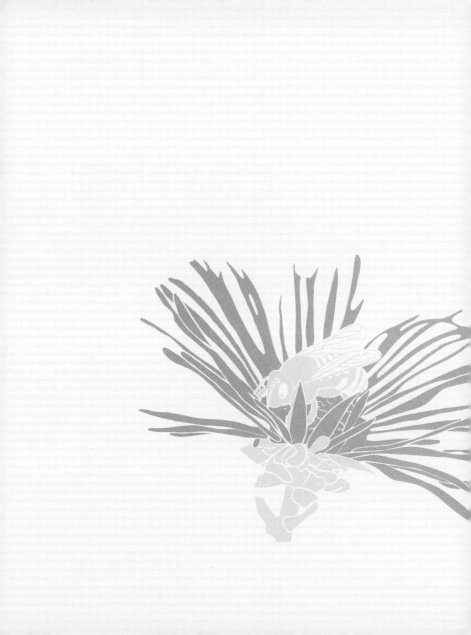

Impatient Gardener's
Question Time

Q *I'm an impatient gardener looking for a quick fix. A water feature doesn't sound very quick to me.*

A That's where you're wrong. You could make a barrel pond on the patio in no time at all. Put a layer of gravel or pebbles in the bottom of a watertight wooden barrel, add a couple of aquatic plants in their plastic baskets plus a bunch of oxygenating weed, and fill with water. Just make sure the barrel is at least 30cm (12in) deep. You could do the same thing using a big glazed pot without a drainage hole.

Even simpler, fill a large shallow bowl with water, add a few iridescent glass nuggets for some sparkle and stand it in a sunny position on your patio.

Or if you're a bird lover, just add a bird bath to the garden, sit back and enjoy.

For moving water, though, you'll have to have an outdoor electricity supply on a separate circuit – and for that you'll have to call on the services of a professional electrician. Do it yourself and you're breaking the law.

Pool your ideas

* In an informal garden go for a natural-looking pool. You can buy pre-formed fibreglass liners but they give an unnatural shape. Far better to use a flexible pond liner and give your pond generous free-flowing curves rather than lots of fiddly ins and outs.

* Dense planting helps to blur the edges of the pool and make it blend in with its surroundings in a naturalistic way.

* If you plan to keep fish, your pool must be at least 60cm (24in) deep so the fish are safe from predatory birds and from ice if the water freezes in winter.

* A shelf around the side of the pool about 30cm (12in) down enables you to grow attractive marginal plants in baskets as well as deep-water plants and oxygenators to keep the water healthy.

* A formal pool should be a strong geometric shape – square, rectangular or circular. The geometry is important in a formal setting so it's best to leave the pool unplanted. This will give the best reflective quality to the water too. To enhance this, either use a black pond liner or have the inside of the pool rendered and painted with black pond paint.

Big and bold

Be bold with pools and make them as large as possible. The impact they make is so much greater and, besides, large pools are easier to maintain.

Impatient Gardener's Question Time

Q *I've had the electrics done but before I buy a pump, what sort of water-feature options are there for me to consider?*

A There's lots of choice depending on your taste and budget. You can buy a ready-made water feature such as an old-fashioned hand pump pouring water into a barrel, which is fun in a country-style garden, or a wall fountain, which suits a formal garden.

You could install a bubble fountain. Dig a hole for the reservoir and pump. Once they're in place, cover the lid of the reservoir with pebbles, stone chippings, crushed glass or florists' nuggets, turn on the power and off you go.

Or you could install a large metal or glass sphere over a reservoir. The sphere is hollow and when the water is pumped up through it, surface tension makes the water cling to the sides. The surface of the sphere comes alive with the subtle movement of the water catching the light.

Three ideas to keep you on the level

1 Try rills or channels, no more than 25cm (10in) wide or deep, dissecting the garden. This idea originated thousands of years ago in Persian 'paradise gardens'. The Persians believed the universe was divided into four quarters, so the earliest paradise gardens were divided into four by rills. Your rills could run parallel or could intersect. Each would need its own reservoir and pump to keep the water flowing.

2 Make a much broader rill and fill it with rows of widely spaced setts so the water flows between them. Although it would look as though you were walking on water, in fact your feet would remain dry.

3 In a modern garden, try small oblong or cross-shaped pools set into smooth concrete or resinated aggregate and lined with aluminium. The effect is stunning.

Chute to kill

A stainless-steel chute or a reinforced steel joist set in a smooth rendered wall, pouring a sheet of water into a slender rectangular pool looks very striking in a contemporary setting.

FEATURES

Did you know that...?

... features are the finishing touches that give a garden personality. More than anything else, they can stamp your personality on the garden, distil its essence and create a mood. For the impatient gardener, they are ideal because all that is required in most instances is a bit of careful thought about where to place them to best advantage.

Don't break the bank

The type of feature you choose depends not only on the style of your garden but on your bank balance. Antique stone classical figures are very expensive – too expensive to risk leaving outside – but there are good-quality reproductions available, which make very acceptable alternatives. There are also less expensive, slightly rougher concrete versions made from moulds. These would work well in a less formal setting, especially after a bit of 'distressing' (see page 143) and if you position them among the plants.

Impatient Gardener's Question Time

Q *I love antique stone and think it would suit my garden style, but I've had a look and don't think my purse will stretch to a big piece like a statue. Apart from reproduction stone, are there any other alternatives?*

A If you're determined to have a piece of antique stone, investigate architectural salvage yards for ornate finials, broken pediments, chunks of column or even pieces of statue – a severed head or maybe a pair of feet. These can look very good, especially if you stand them on a plinth.

Ring the changes

Garden features, whatever they're made of, change according to the light at different times of day and different times of year. They will also be a different colour wet or dry and, if they are placed among plants, will assume more or less prominence according to the season.

Pure abstraction

Abstract sculpture can work well in any
style of garden, depending on the material
and how the piece is displayed. A beautiful,
smooth, crafted metal, wood or stone piece
displayed on a simple plinth would work
equally well in a traditional formal garden
or a modern one. A more free-form,
angular or organic piece would be better
in an informal or modern setting.

Animal farm

Animal sculptures – bronze geese, chicken-wire sheep, even rusting metal hippos – can also work well, but they must be aesthetically pleasing in their own right and/or great fun. You may think rabbits pushing wheelbarrows, hedgehogs on their hind legs or 'mooning' gnomes fall into this category. I couldn't possibly comment.

Special commission

If you can't find exactly the sort of feature you want, contact a local sculptor – perhaps through your local art college – and commission a piece. It need not be prohibitively expensive unless the sculptor is famous. You'll end up with something that suits both your personality and your garden.

Formal...

🍀 In a formal garden, a sculpture looks best against a simple background such as a hedge or a wall covered in evergreen climbers. That way its contours stand out very clearly.

🍀 Placing any sculptural object on a plinth immediately gives it a much more formal, thought-out look.

...meets informal...

🍀 In a more informal setting, sculpture is most effective among planting, where its solidity and artifice contrast beautifully with the foliage around it. In Vita Sackville West's famous white garden at Sissinghurst, Kent, for example, a pale grey lead statue of a vestal virgin stands under the canopy of a silver weeping pear.

* Placing a sculptural object on the ground produces an informal effect – and adds an element of surprise.

...somewhere between

* Natural materials such as pieces of driftwood, bleached and worn by the sea, look fantastic in a natural setting where they appear to be part of the landscape. But put them in a formal or modern setting and the contrast between nature and artifice has an even more powerful effect.

Rock on

* Jagged pieces of rock work very well in an oriental-style or modern garden. Place them on a patio or in a gravel garden, either lying flat or standing upright, when they will resemble ancient standing stones.

* Large, smooth boulders are effective too, either on hard landscaping to contrast with the geometry of the paving, or among planting where their contours enhance the shapes and texture of the leaves.

Six garden features to go

1 A group of tall stainless-steel spirals – sold as tomato supports – can look stunning in a modern setting.

2 Solar panels move in the wind and can be wired to a battery to provide power to operate a water feature or some garden lighting, thereby adding function to form.

3 Old horticultural and agricultural implements are worth looking out for. Many, though, like old millstones, ploughs or watering cans, now have antique status and a price tag to match.

4 Industrial machine parts are often surprisingly beautiful. Old grinding wheels or cogs look strikingly architectural on top of a wall, whether an old brick wall or a modern rendered one.

5 Ball bearings come in a range of sizes, up to 1m (36in) in diameter. These make perfect stainless-steel spheres to stand on the paving in a minimalist garden.

6 Old CDs make great mobiles, hanging from trees and sending shafts of light darting all round the garden. They are also good for keeping the birds off edible crops, so they are functional too.

PLANT MAGIC

Can't wait, won't wait?

* If you're an impatient gardener you want to start getting pleasure from your garden straight away, whatever the time of year, so get planting and be bold.

* For maximum drama, use loads of the same plant and put them all together – fifty narcissi in a huge clump look far better than ten dotted all around.

* For maximum impact, stick to one or, at most, two colours.

* For maximum enjoyment, plant in a spot that you can see from the house – from the kitchen or dining window, or through the patio doors.

* If it's winter, plant in containers – a mass of pale green-and-white ornamental cabbages or the brightly variegated evergreen *Euonymus fortunei* 'Emerald 'n' Gold'.

* In summer make the most of annuals – and add some height with a forest of tall sunflowers or a mass of beautiful scented *Nicotiana sylvestris*.

* While you're waiting for your hardy annuals to flower, place a large pot among them, planted with bright spring bedding – forget-me-nots, pink and white daisies (*Bellis*) or some wallflowers.

Lasting pleasure, minimal effort

Here's a sizzling purple and yellow planting idea that will give you instant gratification in the winter as well as a display in spring and early summer.

* Clear an area at least 60 x 30cm (24 x 12in). Plant a minimum of a dozen mid-season yellow tulips per 30cm (12in) square, each tulip evenly spaced, not touching the next and in a hole at least three times its own depth. Fill in around the bulbs with soil, then plant a mixture of purple winter-flowering pansies and rich blue forget-me-nots on top. Don't worry about leaving room for the tulips – they'll find space to push up through.

* As long as there is some sunlight, the pansies should flower right through the winter and well into the spring when the tulips and forget-me-nots will come into flower.

Climbers

Grown up obelisks or wigwams, climbers can give height far more quickly than any other plants, and they can brighten up walls and fences too. They are also invaluable for adding interest to existing shrubs or hedges that are serviceable but dull. These will give a good show even in the first year that you plant them.

In my plant portraits ☆ is used to show a Temporary Star, a plant that can be removed once surrounding plants have reached a decent size. ◯ is used to show a Stayer, a plant to enjoy for many years.

Clematis armandii

SIZE AFTER ONE SEASON:
1.8 x 1.8m
(6 x 6ft)

ULTIMATE SIZE:
7.5 x 7.5m
(25 x 25ft)

This evergreen clematis is a handsome plant for a town garden, producing long slender leathery leaves and masses of white (C. a. 'Snowdrift') or blush-white (C. a. 'Apple Blossom') flowers in spring, which are also scented. It is good trained up and along the top of a wall or allowed to scramble through an old tree. Although it is hardy down to −15°C (5°F), it does best with some protection from cold winds. Like all clematis, it is happiest with its head in the sun and its roots in the shade. It tolerates both acid and alkaline soil, but prefers it to be well drained but moisture-retentive. It climbs by means of tendrils, so give it something to latch onto such as a grid of wire. It needs no pruning unless it outgrows its allotted space, though some older stems can be shortened to encourage more vigorous new growth.

Passiflora caerulea
Passionflower

SIZE AFTER ONE SEASON:
2 x 2m
(6ft 6in x 6ft 6in)

ULTIMATE SIZE:
6 x 6m
(20 x 20ft)

This is a vigorous climber with attractive hand-shaped leaves and curious white, purple and blue flowers from midsummer to autumn. It also has fruit in late summer and autumn. It is a rambler and is best trained over wires or trellis. It loses its leaves in winter and the top growth can be killed off in very cold weather, but in most cases it will produce new growth in the spring. Where space is confined, it can be cut hard back to within 1m (3ft 3in) or so of ground level in early spring and will quickly regrow. It does best in full sun but can tolerate light shade, and can cope with all soil types except very dry or very limy ones.

Solanum jasminoides 'Album'
White potato vine

**SIZE AFTER
ONE SEASON:
2.5 x 2.5m
(8 x 8ft)**

**ULTIMATE SIZE:
5 x 5m
(16 x 16ft)**

This vigorous white-flowered relative of the potato vine is ideal for growing up and over a pergola or a tree. It has attractive mid-green leaves that are evergreen in sheltered town gardens, and clusters of small white flowers with bright yellow stamens from late spring to early autumn. It is happy in most soils, except extremely dry ones, and will grow in full sun to medium shade. It is not reliably hardy in cold or exposed gardens. It is a twiner, so give it a framework of wires or stout trellis to scramble up. On a pergola, it is best to wrap the uprights with chicken wire to give it a good start.

Three quick fixes for a shady side passageway

1 For an informal look, paint the walls or fences a very pale colour and freshen up the floor with masonry paint, pale chippings or pale grey decking. Add trellis to the walls and hang pots of ferns, fuchsias, lobelia or tuberous begonias from it. Along the base of the wall, use deep troughs planted with hostas and more ferns and, if you want climbers, choose a brightly variegated evergreen ivy such as *Hedera helix* 'Oro di Bogliasco' (syn. *H. h.* 'Goldheart') or *H. h.* 'Glacier'.

2 For a formal look, decorate with evergreen box balls, lollipops or spirals in square tubs or simple terracotta pots. Add a few pots of hostas, or alternating pots of mind-your-own-business (*Soleirolia soleirolii*) in light green and dark green or some white busy lizzies.

3 For a modern look, paint the walls ochre, pale terracotta or turquoise and fix shelves to the walls with stainless-steel shop fittings. Use bright plastic or metal containers and bold planting – huge-leafed hostas and New Guinea hybrid busy lizzies in hot tropical scarlet, orange or magenta.

Shrubs

In small spaces you need to choose shrubs that will earn their keep either by having attractive foliage, a very long flowering period or several seasons of interest – flowers and attractive berries in winter, perhaps, or vibrant autumn colour. These are good value, even in their first year, and will go on getting even better.

Lavatera 'Barnsley'
Shrubby mallow

**SIZE AFTER
ONE SEASON:
1.5 x 1m
(5ft x 3ft 3in)**

**ULTIMATE SIZE:
2 x 2m
(6ft 6in x 6ft 6in)**

This shrub is an excellent temporary
space-filler, producing masses of open
white flowers with a red eye from early
summer to the first frosts. It also has grey-
green medium-sized leaves, which are a
good foil for the showier flowers. Lavatera
is best cut back in the spring, removing
all the wood that carried flowers the
previous summer, to keep it in check and
to encourage better flowering. After a few
years, though, it has a tendency to sprawl
untidily, so take it out.

Cornus alba 'Elegantissima' Dogwood

SIZE AFTER ONE SEASON:
1.5 x 1.2m
(5 x 4ft)

ULTIMATE SIZE:
3 x 4m
(10 x 13ft)

Dogwoods are useful shrubs for small gardens since they have more than one season of interest and can easily be kept in check. They are grown primarily for their winter bark, which in this case is rich ruby-red. In spring and summer it has pale green-and-white variegated leaves, which make it a very good background plant for other shrubs or perennials, or even a host for a small-flowered clematis. Since the brightest coloured bark is produced by the previous summer's new growth, cut it hard back to about 15cm (6in) from the ground every spring. This also encourages larger, more strikingly variegated leaves as well as restricting the shrub's overall size. It does well on all soils, including boggy ones, and will cope with full sun to medium shade.

Ceanothus 'Puget Blue'
Californian lilac

SIZE AFTER
ONE SEASON:
1.5 x 1.2m
(5 x 4ft)

ULTIMATE SIZE:
3 x 3m
(10 x 10ft)

A good structural evergreen shrub with dark green leaves, it is smothered in rich blue flowers in late spring to early summer. It prefers full sun but will tolerate light shade and needs a deep rich soil to do well. It dislikes poor, alkaline soil. For additional enjoyment, grow a late-flowering clematis such as C. 'Alba Luxurians' or C. *viticella* 'Purpurea Plena Elegans' through it. After flowering, you can trim back the wood that has borne flowers, but it does not respond well to hard pruning. Ceanothus tends to be short-lived, often dying after about ten years.

Setting standards

If you've inherited an overgrown back garden with some big old shrubs that are taking up too much room, rather than ripping them out, try 'standardizing' them – removing the lower branches so that you are left with a bare trunk and growth at the top, like a tree, and more space below.

Herbaceous perennials

Many herbaceous perennials, especially those that flower in late summer and early autumn, give a good show in their first season. For immediate impact, grow three, five or, if space allows, seven plants of the same type in a group.

Knautia macedonica
Plume poppy

SIZE AFTER ONE SEASON:
1.8m x 60cm
(6 x 2ft)

This plant, with its wine-red clover-like flowers, is very fashionable and deservedly so because it flowers for months in the summer. To keep it a good compact shape, grow it in well-drained, not-too-fertile soil and in full sun.

Cynara cardunculus
Cardoon

**SIZE AFTER
ONE SEASON:
2.5 x 1.2m
(8 x 4ft)**

This relative of the artichoke makes a dramatic temporary miniature tree substitute, with huge jagged silver leaves up to 60cm (24in) long and vivid purple thistle flowers in summer, about the size of a grapefruit. It dies down in autumn, but will produce fresh growth the following spring. Since it takes up a lot of room, in a small space it is probably most useful as a one-season wonder. It prefers a sunny position and fertile well-drained soil and, because of its height, it needs shelter from strong winds.

Artemisia absinthium 'Lambrook Silver'

**SIZE AFTER
ONE SEASON:**
45 x 45cm
(18 x 18in)

ULTIMATE SIZE:
60 x 60cm
(2 x 2ft)

This is a superb foliage plant for a sunny border. With its very finely divided bright silver foliage it is an ideal foil both for soft pastels and for 'hot' shades. Unlike other artemisias, which have rather dirty yellow flowers that are best cut off when the buds appear, this has tiny grey flowers that you do not really notice. It likes a well-drained but not dry soil and full sun. If you cut it back hard in spring, you will be rewarded with new, even brighter silver foliage.

☆ *Crambe cordifolia*

**SIZE AFTER
ONE SEASON:**
1.8 x 1m
(6ft x 3ft 3in)

ULTIMATE SIZE:
2.5 x 1.5m
(8 x 5ft)

Another huge dramatic plant, which produces a massive cloud of tiny fragrant white flowers from a clump of large architectural deep green leaves. Bees love it. It is best as a temporary plant in a small border, though lovely with roses where there is more space.

Ground-cover plants

These spread quickly to cover the soil, which not only gives a new garden a mature look, but also helps suppress weeds. They are best planted in groups of three, five or seven. They will soon knit together to form an impenetrable carpet.

Campanula poscharskyana 'E.H. Frost'

SIZE AND SPREAD AFTER ONE SEASON:
15 x 40cm
(6 x 16in)

ULTIMATE SIZE:
20cm x 1m
(8in x 3ft 3in)

This forms mounds of fresh green leaves from which long growths are produced that cover the ground very quickly but give it a reputation for invasiveness. However, it is very easily controlled by simply pulling off the growths when they have gone too far. It grows in sun or part-shade, and in most soil types except very boggy ones. It will also grow in cracks in paving or walls.

Galium odoratum
Woodruff

**SIZE AFTER
ONE SEASON:**
15 x 45cm
(6 x 18in)

ULTIMATE SIZE:
15cm x indefinite
(6in x indefinite)

This excellent ground-cover plant grows very quickly sideways, soon forming a carpet of pretty, fresh, green lobed leaves. It is usually deciduous, but in my own garden it keeps its leaves all winter. In late spring and early summer it has scented white starry flowers. It will carry on spreading, so either give it plenty of room or chop it back with a spade when it over-reaches itself. As a woodland plant it likes moist soil and dappled shade. It is good used formally, in a circular brick-edged bed for instance, or informally as weed-suppressing ground cover under shrubs or trees.

Grasses

A brilliant group of plants for the impatient gardener because they grow very quickly but, except in a few cases, are not invasive. They have a very long season of interest – even the dead stems of deciduous grasses look great in winter – and they are also good in containers.

Calamagrostis x *acutiflora* 'Karl Foerster'

**SIZE AFTER
ONE SEASON:**
1.8m x 30cm
(6 x 1ft)

ULTIMATE SIZE:
1.8m x 60cm
(6 x 2ft)

This very upright grass with fine mid-green leaves is excellent for providing height without bulk. In early summer it has brownish-pink flowers that gradually fade to buff. The dead stems and foliage turn an attractive pale gold and give valuable structure through the winter. They look marvellous with the frost on them, illuminated by the low winter sun. Cut back the dead growth as soon as new shoots start appearing in early spring.

Miscanthus sinensis 'Silberfeder'

SIZE AFTER ONE SEASON:
2m x 30cm
(6ft 6in x 1ft)

ULTIMATE SIZE:
2.5 x 1.2m
(8 x 4ft)

An attractive grass with slender arching mid-green leaves, this produces upright silvery flower heads in late summer/early autumn, which stay on the plant through the winter and add valuable structure to the garden. Cut all the dead growth down in early spring. Miscanthus prefers sun and a moist but free-draining soil. It can cope with drier soil but does not thrive when it is too wet.

Stipa arundinacea

**SIZE AFTER
ONE SEASON:**
60 x 60cm
(2 x 2ft)

ULTIMATE SIZE:
1 x 1.2m
(3ft 3in x 4ft)

This is a very striking evergreen grass that makes a wonderful fountain of orange-streaked bright green leaves, with clouds of fine coppery seed heads from midsummer to early autumn. It colours best in a sunny position but will do well in shade. It is happy in most soils except heavy wet ones. It is also superb in a large pot as a focal point.

Bulbs

These are great for impatient gardeners because you can buy many of them already in flower in pots and can see immediately what you are getting. Remove the clump carefully from its pot and plant it in the ground or in a decorative container, or simply bury the pot and then, once the flowering is over, plant the bulbs in the soil. Or plant spring-flowering bulbs in autumn for a great show a few months later.

Allium christophii

**SIZE AFTER
ONE SEASON:**
60 x 15cm
(2ft x 6in)

ULTIMATE SIZE:
60 x 15cm
(2ft x 6in)

Alliums certainly add drama to any border. This particular variety produces long slender stems supporting large heads the size of a grapefruit in late spring and early summer. The heads are made up of masses of small, silvery-mauve star-like flowers. Once the flowers die, the heads fade to a soft biscuit colour. They are very attractive still, so are well worth leaving on the plant until they crumble. These alliums need a reasonably free-draining soil and a sunny position. They take up very little ground space, so are ideal for growing among other plants.

Iris reticulata

SIZE AFTER ONE SEASON:
10–15 x 5cm
(4–6 x 2in)

This is a very attractive miniature iris with deep blue velvety flowers with a splash of gold on each petal. It can start flowering as early as January. It looks terrific growing through low ground-cover plants such as epimedium or evergreen vinca. It is also very attractive en masse in pots.

Narcissus 'Hawera'

SIZE IN ONE SEASON:
25 x 7.5cm
(10 x 3in)

There are many superb dwarf daffodils suitable for small gardens or containers, but this is one of my favourites, producing nodding clusters of canary-yellow flowers in late spring. Plant en masse for the best effect and leave the foliage to die down for six weeks after flowering is over, so that it can manufacture food for the bulb to produce next year's flowers. Planting these daffodils under deciduous shrubs or among perennials will hide the dying foliage or at least distract the eye.

Annuals

Annuals grow, flower, set seed and die in one season and so are great for quick and easy colour in a new garden, or in existing borders that are lacking cohesion. Hardy annuals, which are sown directly into the soil, are very easy to grow and can be in flower in 10–12 weeks. You can buy half-hardy annuals as plants, but they should not go outside until all danger of frost has past.

Calendula 'Indian Prince'
Pot marigold

SIZE IN ONE SEASON:
45–60 x 25cm
(18–24in x 10in)

One of the very fastest annuals to flower from seed – about eight weeks – this is a cottage-garden favourite. This variety has deep orange flowers and looks marvellous on its own or grown with deep blues such as love-in-a-mist or cornflowers. Its flowers are edible and add a real visual zing to any salad. It self-seeds very easily.

Wigwam effect

Make a tall wigwam of copper piping tied at the top with a leather thong or strong jute and stand it in the border. This will become a dramatic focal point straight away. Around the base, sow bright orange California poppy (*Eschscholzia californica*) seed. Once all danger of frost is past, plant rich blue morning glories (*Ipomoea tricolor* 'Heavenly Blue'), bought as young plants from the garden centre, at the base of each leg, and encourage them to latch on. By midsummer they should be producing a profusion of lovely trumpet flowers, each one lasting only for a morning – hence the plant's common name.

Helianthus annuus
Sunflower

SIZE IN ONE SEASON
2m x 30cm
(6ft 6in x 1ft)

The best fast annual there is and, grown en masse, it is a great and stylish space filler. As well as the classic giant yellow variety, look for the rich mahogany *H. a.* 'Velvet Queen', or the very pale lemon *H. a.* 'Italian White', both slightly smaller at around 1.5m (5ft). Sow the seeds directly in soil or in compost in a large pot in mid-spring.

Nigella damascena 'Miss Jekyll'
Love-in-a-mist

SIZE IN ONE
SEASON:
45 x 15cm
(18 x 6in)

This is one of the best and easiest hardy annuals with very fine feathery foliage and rich blue flowers, followed by biscuit-brown seed capsules that look like precious stones in an ornate filigree setting. It likes a sunny position. Another rampant self-seeder, it can be sown in autumn for an earlier show the following year.

Basket case

If you have an old tree in your garden, one very quick and easy way of brightening up the whole area is to suspend several hanging baskets from the branches. For maximum impact, make the baskets identical and stick to a limited colour range. This colour scheme is orange and yellow.

Line a 35-cm (14-in) plastic-coated wire basket with moss and fill with soil-less compost mixed with water-retaining gel crystals and controlled-release fertilizer. Plant with three *Lysimachia nummularia* 'Aurea', three *Lysimachia congestiflora* 'Outback Sunset'®, three *Bidens ferulifolia*, five *Zinnia* 'Profusion Orange' and ten nasturtium plants – *Tropaeolum majus* 'Tip Top Apricot'. In addition, push ten or so nasturtium seeds into the compost. These will start flowering later in the summer and will help keep the whole glorious display going for longer. Finally, at the centre use a foliage plant – *Artemisia vulgaris* 'Oriental Limelight'. Water every day and twice a day in hot weather.

Instant plants

These plants are worth buying as large mature specimens because they will establish well and give your garden instant height and drama.

Hosta sieboldiana var. *elegans*

SIZE AFTER 2/3 SEASONS:
45 x 45cm
(18 x 18in)

ULTIMATE SIZE:
1 x 1.2m
(3ft 3in x 4ft)

Of the hundreds of hostas available, this is one of the most spectacular, with its huge rounded, ribbed blue-green leaves and tall spikes of pale lilac flowers in early summer. One large plant or a matching pair make a stunning, instant feature. It likes deep rich soil that never dries out and will grow in sun or part-shade. The more moisture it has, the more sun it can take.

Phyllostachys nigra
Black bamboo

A large specimen of this bamboo makes an eye-catching focal point or screen.

Pyracantha
Firethorn

SIZE AFTER 2/3 SEASONS:
2 x 1.2m
(6ft 6in x 4ft)

ULTIMATE SIZE:
4 x 3m
(13 x 10ft)

This useful evergreen wall shrub can be bought ready-trained flat on trellis. It is very useful for a shady position, with a long season of interest. It has attractive shiny evergreen leaves all year, pretty white flowers in early summer and then clusters of berries in yellow, orange or scarlet in autumn and winter – or until the birds get them. It is happy in everything from full sun to deep shade, although it will flower less freely in the latter, but it dislikes very exposed positions.

KEEPING
IT GOING

Impatient Gardener's Question Time

Q *I'm an impatient gardener, so time is precious and I'd rather entertain, relax or sit in my garden than slave away in it. How can I avoid all those tedious garden chores?*

A The trick is to identify the routine tasks that take up most time, and either eliminate them altogether, or reduce them to a bare minimum.

Seven tips to minimize weeding

1 As with so many things, prevention is better than cure. If you are planting a garden from scratch, dig the soil over very thoroughly and remove every scrap of weed root. Many weeds will grow from even a millimetre of root. Remember the old saying, 'One year's seed, seven years' weeds'. Remove weeds before they set seed.

2 If the problem starts in a neighbouring garden, you need to make a barrier. Dig a trench about 30cm (12in) deep along the base of the fence on your side, then nail a 30cm (12in) wide strip of thick black polythene along the bottom of the fence and push it down into the trench. This will prevent most perennial weeds from creeping under the fence and into your garden.

3 Mulch. Once the soil is as free from perennial weeds as possible, keep them at bay by covering the soil with a layer of mulch.

4 Choose either an organic material such as compost, cocoa shells or composted bark, or an inorganic mulch of gravel, stone chippings or even crushed glass.

5 Alternatively, lay a woven membrane over the soil and cover this with a purely ornamental layer of gravel or bark.

6 Use ground-cover plants. In the longer term these are an attractive way of keeping weeds under control.

7 As a last resort, if you don't want to do the weeding yourself, get an experienced gardener in.

Four tips to minimize watering

1 Mulch (again!) Apply a mulch when the soil is already moist and it will help keep moisture in.

2 Install an automatic watering system. The simplest consists of a soaker hose – a porous pipe that slowly seeps water along its entire length. Lay it permanently on the soil around the base of shrubs and trees and weave it in and out of the smaller plants. You can cover it with soil or with a mulch. Attach it to a water computer fixed to an outside tap to set watering times.

3 For containers you need a micro-irrigation system – a feeder hose into which much narrower plastic pipes are fixed. These have either a drip feeder or a small spray on a spike at the other end. The spikes are then pushed into the soil and the water is delivered exactly where it is needed. This system can also be controlled by a water computer.

4 Reduce the amount of watering needed by plants in containers by mixing water-retaining gel crystals into the compost as you plant. These are able to hold many times their own volume of water, which they then release gradually into the compost.

Feed me

* For a garden you are starting from scratch, dig in some decent organic matter such as well-rotted manure or garden compost. Use only one shovelful of manure every square metre (3ft), and two shovelfuls of compost. Adding a little bit extra in the hope of making your plants grow even faster will only produce lots of soft sappy growth that is prone to all sorts of pests and diseases.

* If you are planting in an existing border, mix organic matter into the soil at the bottom of the planting hole and into the soil with which you refill the hole.

❀ If you are not concerned about being organic, you can use an inorganic fertiliser. The easiest to use are controlled-release fertilizers that last a whole season and can be used in borders or for containers. These come as granules or thimble-shaped plugs that you simply push into the soil or into the compost in your containers. The coating of the granules is heat-sensitive. The granules only start to release their nutrients when the soil or compost warms up and the plants start to grow and need feeding, so you can also use them if you plant in autumn.

Impatient Gardener's Question Time

Q *Do I really have to do all that pruning stuff I've read about in books?*

A Pruning isn't that difficult, but it helps to understand why you need to prune. First of all, it keeps plants within the space allotted to them. You could grow only plants that will remain very small, but that would be boring. For the sake of fifteen minutes or so once a year – all it takes to prune most plants – isn't it more fun to grow some bigger, much more exciting specimens and keep them under control?

The second reason for pruning is that it removes some of the old tired wood. Most shrubs flower more freely on younger wood and produce larger flowers too. And for shrubs that feature coloured leaves and bark, pruning will produce bigger and more intensely coloured leaves and brighter bark.

Q *But isn't there a risk I'll kill the plants?*

A It's very hard to kill a plant by pruning it. Tests have shown that even if you prune a rose with a hedge trimmer from time to time, it will still flower well though it may not be a beautiful shape. Mostly, the worst that is likely to happen is that if you prune at the wrong time of year you will lose that season's flowers.

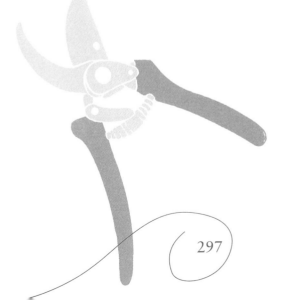

All you need to know to prune spring and early-summer flowerers

❀ These flower on growth they made the previous summer, so they need to be pruned immediately they have finished flowering.

❀ They will spend the rest of the summer producing the wood on which next year's flowers will form.

❀ Cut back all of the growth that has borne flowers to the point from which a healthy new shoot is emerging.

All you need to know to prune plants that flower from midsummer onwards

* These produce flowers on growth made this year, so the old growth needs to be pruned back hard in late autumn after flowering or, better still, in very early spring just as the plants start growing.

* If you don't prune, you will get flowers high up, on the new season's growth, and the flowers will be smaller and fewer too.

All you need to know about pruning roses

✿ Just remove any dead, diseased or very weak and spindly growth.

✿ When you deadhead, always remove 15–20cm (6–8in) of stem at the same time. This helps to keep the rose in check.

* Cut out an older stem or two right down to ground level in early spring every few years to encourage strong new growth from the base.

* And best of all, avoid planting roses that need extensive annual pruning – primarily the hybrid teas or floribundas. Instead choose more easily maintained types such as modern shrub roses, English roses and patio roses.

Index

Acaena microphylla 'Copper Carpet' 95
Allium christophii 273
aluminium chippings 110
annuals 247, 276–81
aquatic plants 131
arches and arbours 176–95
architectural plants 151, 174
Armeria maritima 94
Artemisia absinthium 'Lambrook Silver' 264
   A. vulgaris 'Oriental Limelight' 283

bamboo, black 285
bamboo screens 43–5
barrel ponds 214
baskets 142, 282–3
benches 207
Bidens ferulifolia 283
bird baths 215
boundaries 7–49
brick: edging lawns 117
   pavers 78, 99, 100, 117
   pergolas 186
   surfaces 98–100
   walls 16, 37
bubble fountains 172, 220
bulbs 124, 272–5
busy lizzies 255

cabbages, ornamental 247
Calamagrostis x *acutiflora* 'Karl Foerster' 269
Calendula 'Indian Prince' 277
Californian lilac 259
Campanula poscharskyana

'E.H. Frost' 266
cardoons 263
carpeting plants 94–5, 118, 266–7, 291
Ceanothus 'Puget Blue' 259
ceramic pots 140
chairs 201–9
chamomile lawns 118
Clematis armandii 251
climbing plants 181, 250–3, 254, 279
close-boarded fences 46
cobbles 78
colour: container plants 148
   furniture 204, 207
   gravel 106
   painting walls 24–5
   plants 246
   sheds and summerhouses 196–7
   stone slabs 84
   wood stains 28–9, 70–1
composts, in containers 132, 138
concrete: painting slabs 72–7
   patios 66
   poured concrete surfaces 97
   walls 38–9
containers 121–55
   aquatic plants 131
   bulbs 124
   colour schemes 148
   compost 132, 138
   drainage 138
   edible plants 129, 135
   grouping 137
   herbs 135, 154–5
   materials 140–5
   planting 146–7, 151, 247
   positioning 150

size 136, 137
tender plants 127
topiary 152, 255
trees in 126, 129
watering 293
Cornus alba 'Elegantissima' 258
Crambe cordifolia 265
crazy paving 89
curved walls 39
Cynara cardunculus 263
Cyperus papyrus 141

daffodils 275
daisies 247
decking 62, 65–71
dogwood 258
drainage, containers 138

eating areas 169
Echeveria elegans 76
electricity: lighting 160, 165
   water features 215, 220
Eschscholzia californica 279
Euonymus fortunei 'Emerald 'n' Gold' 247

features 227–43
fences 7–10
   bamboo screens 43–5
   close-boarded fences 46
   contemporary style 40, 47
   covering 30
   finials 34
   painting 28–9, 32–3
ferns 254
fertilizers 295
finials, fence posts 34
firethorn 285
fish 216
forget-me-nots 247, 249

fountains 172, 220
frost protection 127
fruit trees, in containers 129
furniture 199–209

Galium odoratum 267
gazebos 178
glass: containers 141
    crushed glass 110
    marbles 79, 215
granite setts 102
grass, lawns 56–9, 112–19
grasses 268–71
gravel 105–9
ground-cover plants 94–5,
    266–7, 291

hard landscaping 56–60
Hedera helix 254
Helianthus annuus 280
herbs 135, 154–5
Hosta 254, 255
    H. sieboldiana var. *elegans*
        284

internal divisions 11, 12, 14,
    18, 21, 39
Ipomoea tricolor 'Heavenly
    Blue' 279
Iris reticulata 274
ivy 254

Knautia macedonica 262

Lavatera 'Barnsley' 257
lawns 56–9, 112–19
lighting 157–75
lilies 124
love-in-a-mist 281
Lysimachia 283

maintenance 287–301
mallow, shrubby 257

marigolds 277
masonry paint 23, 72
Melianthus major 174
metal containers 141
mind-your-own-business 255
mint, Corsican 118
Miscanthus sinensis
    'Silberfeder' 270
morning glory 279
mosaic 79
mowing lawns 117
mulches 291, 292

Narcissus 246
    N. 'Hawera' 275
narrow gardens 12
nasturtiums 283
New Zealand burr 95
Nicotiana sylvestris 247
Nigella damascena 'Miss
    Jekyll' 281

organic matter 294

painting: concrete slabs 72–7
    containers 145
    fences 28–9, 32–3
    sheds and summerhouses
        196–7
    walls 23–5
pansies 249
papyrus 141
passageways, plants for
    254–5
Passiflora caerulea 252
passionflower 252
patios 60, 66
    facelifts 78–9
    painting 72–7
    planting in 92
    stone 80–91

paving see concrete slabs;
    patios
perennials 262–5
pergolas 178, 181, 182, 184,
    186–9
Phyllostachys nigra 285
planting: containers 146–7,
    151, 247
    in patios 92
    pools 216, 217
plants 245–85
plume poppy 262
ponds and pools: barrel
    ponds 214
    formal pools 217
    lighting 163, 172
    liners 216
    planting 216, 217
    size 219
    water chutes 224
poppy, California 279
posts, fence 34, 40
potato vine 253
pressure washer 72
privacy 182
pruning 296–301
Pyracantha 285

rills 21, 223
rocks 241
rope: bamboo screens 44–5
    pergolas 187
roses, pruning 297, 300–1

salad plants 135
screens 14–15, 17, 43–5
sculpture 234–9
security lighting 166
setts, granite 102
shade, plants for 254–5
shadows, lighting and 174

sheds 196
shrubs 256–60
  in containers 129
  pruning 296
  topiary 152
slabs see concrete slabs; stone
sloping gardens 65
soil: in containers 132, 138
  improving 294–5
  mulches 291, 292
Solanum jasminoides 'Album'
  253
Soleirolia soleirolii 255
Stachys byzantina 'Silver
  Carpet' 95
'standardizing' shrubs 260
statues 168, 230, 238
stencils 75
stepping stones 117

Stipa arundinacea 271
stone: containers 142–3
  edging lawns 117
  features 231
  patios 80–91
  pergolas 186
summerhouses 197
sunflowers 247, 280
surfaces 50–119

tables 202–7
tender plants 127
terracotta containers 144–5
thrift 94
thyme 94, 118
timber: containers 140
  decking 62, 65–71
  furniture 202–3, 206–7
  pergolas 186, 187–8
  wood stains 28–9, 70–1

  see also fences
topiary 152, 255
trees: in containers 126, 129
  hanging baskets in 282
  lighting 169
trellis 48, 193
Tropaeolum majus 'Tip Top
  Apricot' 283
tulips 249
turf 112, 114–15

urns 142–3, 168

vegetables 135

wallflowers 247
walls 7–10
  brick walls 16, 37
  concrete walls 38–9
  disguising ugly walls 23

Editorial Director Jane O'Shea
Art Director Helen Lewis
Designer Claire Peters
Project Editor Hilary Mandleberg
Production Bridget Fish
Illustrations Hannah McVicar

This edition first published in 2006 by
Quadrille Publishing Limited
Alhambra House, 27–31 Charing Cross Road
London WC2H 0LS

Copyright © Text 2002, 2006 Gay Search
Copyright © Illustrations 2006 Hannah McVicar
Copyright © Design and layout 2006
Quadrille Publishing Ltd

British Library Cataloguing-in-Publication Data
A catalogue record for this book is available from
the British Library.

ISBN-13: 978 184400 272 6
ISBN-10: 1 84400 272 1

Printed in Singapore